Anxiety Disorder
Managing and Overcoming Anxiety Attacks

Dan Miller

Table of Contents

Important Insight

The uneasiness and creeping fear that accompanies anxiety can create a feeling of being trapped in a situation where you cannot unhook yourself. This uneasiness further progresses and combines with panic disorder along the way to finally cripple you emotionally, mentally and physically.

Recent surveys have indicated that between 14 and 18 percent of Europeans and Americans are affected by panic disorders and anxiety.

The question of our age and time is – why are there so many anxiety and panic disorder related cases today and how can we go about it to conquer terror, fear, panic and worry? The answer to this question and many more is the subject matter of this eBook.

It is possible to scale this seemingly insurmountable barrier to our personal happiness and wellness. Undergoing lobotomy or drowning yourself in a bottle of pills may not help much and in extreme cases it may even worsen your situation.

This book discusses the causes and effects of panic and anxiety and the ways in which to manage and overcome mental and physical effects of anxiety. You will also learn how you can stop your mind from generating nightmares thereby giving you relative calm and mental peace.

1: Understanding Anxiety, Fear and Panic Attacks

For you to be able to fully understand the dimensions of anxiety, it is very important to first examine it through the context of other emotional conditions that it is closely associated with. Anxiety is a term derived from the Latin word which means distressed or worried.

According to the World English Dictionary, anxiety refers to a state of uneasiness or tension that is caused by apprehension of possible future misfortunes, danger, worry, etc.

As opposed to fear which occurs in a situation that is at hand, anxiety is more focused on the potential and possibilities of danger before it even happens. For instance, in a situation where a lion or a bear suddenly appears, your reactions as reflected in the steps you take to save yourself are motivated by fear and not anxiety.

Anxiety comes in a situation where you begin thinking about the possibilities of a lion or bear approaching you and then you immediately start pulsating and becoming worried. The event may not have happened but you already feel the effect because your mind has created a scenario of possible danger.

Anxiety is part and parcel of our everyday life whether at school, at our work place or even at home. The feeling of anxiety is almost natural in every human being. However, when the feeling of anxiety crosses the border and affects your sleep, your diet, your relationships and everything else that you do, then it becomes a problem that needs psychology and/or medical attention.

Classifications of Anxiety Disorders

Anxiety disorders are basically psychiatric disorders where you experience chronic anxiety which by normal scales can be termed as unnatural. It is broadly classified into three groups based on the stimuli that trigger the anxiety.

Generalized Anxiety Disorder

This class of anxiety disorder refers to long lasting and non-specific type of anxiety. The people who suffer from this form of anxiety disorder usually exhibit anxiety as they face their day to day tasks. They also have problems in making decisions. For instance, you may feel anxious when deciding on the type of shoe to wear without there being a distinct reason for the anxiety.

Panic Disorder

This refers to a super intensified version of anxiety disorders. It is a psychiatric disorder where you suffer frequent panic attacks. Panic attacks are instances of intense terror that are usually brought about by stressful triggers or at times no triggers at all.

Panic attacks usually happen when you are doing your normal duties or when faced with an extraordinary task ahead of you such as a public speech or a major life decision. As opposed to generalized anxiety, panic attacks are sudden, severe and can paralyze you physically.

Some of the common physical reactions of panic attacks include difficulty in breathing, dizziness, muscle-clenching, shaking and heart palpitations. Some people who suffer from panic attacks usually confuse them with heart attacks.

Phobias

These are disproportional fears which are mainly caused by non-dangerous stimuli. Usually, phobias are linked with panic attacks and anxiety disorders because they attack people in harmless situations. For instance, some people begin to sweat the moment they step into an elevator and nothing can stop them from having that kind of sensation, not even rationalization.

Assessing Your Anxiety Level

There are questionnaires and checklists that you can use to assess your quantitative and qualitative levels of anxiety. These checklists also give you a general idea of the source of your anxiety; whether it stems from generalized anxiety or social anxiety.

The results from these assessments can be discussed and reviewed together with a health practitioner such as a psychiatrist, therapist or psychologist. If you feel that your scores are too low or false then you can seek a second opinion. The following are some of the checklists that you can use.

The Generalized Anxiety Disorder 7 Item Scale (GAD -7)

This scale is a self-screening questionnaire that is commonly used to assess the possibility of generalized anxiety disorder. It has a set of questions with three choices each where you pick the options that you feel represent you based on the frequency you have experienced the sensations listed.

It is important to note that the GAD -7 is just a test to self-assess your generalized anxiety disorder but should not be used as a replacement of clinical assessments. In this scale, if your scores are between 0 and 4 then you have little or no anxiety at all. Where the scores ranges from 6 to 10 then, it implies that you have mild anxiety. A score level of between 11 and 15 means that you have moderate anxiety while severe anxiety is when you attain a score of between 16 and 21.

Zung Self Rating Anxiety Scale

This scale was developed by William W.K. Zung from the Duke University. It is aimed at assessing your quantitative levels of anxiety. It is a questionnaire that is composed of 20 questions that measure anxiety levels based on their effect on your motor, cognitive, autonomic and central nervous systems.

The total scores for this scale range between 20 and 80 points. A score of between 20 and 40 points indicate normal anxiety range, a score of 45 to 59 points signal a mild to moderate anxiety level whereas a score of 60 to 74 points indicate severe anxiety. Finally, if your score ranges from 75 to 80 points then you have a case of extreme anxiety level.

Social Phobia Inventory (SPIN)

Developed at the Dupe University, this questionnaire assesses the magnitude of social anxiety disorder. It has a set of 17 items which have options from A to E. For every answer of A, you get 0 points, B has 1 point, C has 2 Points, D has 3 points and E has 4 points.

The total scores here range from 0 to 68. A score of 0 to 20 signifies little or no social anxiety, a score of 21 to 30 indicates mild social anxiety, 31 to 40 score line shows moderate social anxiety, 41 to 50 points indicate severe social anxiety and ultimately a score lien of between 51 and 68 points is an indication of very severe social anxiety.

There are other surveys and questionnaires still available online that you can use to assess your individual anxiety levels. They cover a wide anxiety spectrum ranging from phobia, panic disorders, agoraphobia and many others.

2: Causes and Symptoms of Anxiety

There are many reasons as to why people suffer from anxiety today. These reasons may range from genetic and hereditary traits to our unique experiences in the world. For some people anxiety comes at a certain age while in others it may gradually develop overtime.

Whatever the case, you are to understand that anxiety is a normal reaction to an instance of stress. For you to be able to address a specific anxiety whether it is generalized anxiety or social anxiety, you have to understand its root cause; the underlying stressor that is responsible for the sensations that you are experiencing.

Causes of Anxiety

Phobias

Phobias are usually associated with anxiety because they arise out of irrational fear. If you experience social phobias and suffer from unwarranted fear you are in a public place then chances are that you are going to develop an anxiety disorder. Some phobias affect us more frequently than others in our day to day lives. For instance, if you have an irrational fear that comes from flying in planes, it may not affect you much if you do not travel frequently. Nearly, all phobias end up in anxiety disorder.

Temporal and Passing Worries

Worries may be legitimate such as concerns over retrenchment, finances, relationships, family and many others. Whenever you accommodate these worries for a long time, then they can snowball into anxiety. Worries result into persistent lack of focus which can significantly lower your productivity which can take you back to the cycle of stress.

Self Esteem Problems

This factor wears heavily on people making them anxious and uncomfortable especially when interacting with others. Self-esteem can either fit as a cause or a symptom of anxiety. People who suffer from low self-esteem usually experience sensations of anxiety whenever they come together in social gatherings and as a consequence tend to avoid such settings. Anxiety due to self-esteem steals from you the joy of life and the sense of accomplishments which can ultimately plunge you into depression.

Substance Abuse

Drug and substance abuse affect the working of the mind. This means that even your emotions are altered making you feel either high or low depending on the kinds of drugs that you take. Depressants for instance are taken to calm the mind making you rather quiet and isolated. When such drugs are taken in exceeding proportions they can lead to depression and ultimately anxiety.

Stimulants on the other hand work on your emotions to make you feel hyper and they can cause anxiety because of the high energy that comes as a result of a stimulated body system. Some of the common substances that can cause anxiety include cannabis, sedatives, alcohol and amphetamines.

Symptoms of Anxiety

There are symptoms that can indicate the presence of anxiety in people. Understanding these symptoms and the context within which they are exhibited can help you in arresting anxiety before it spirals into a major problem. Some of the symptoms include:

Sleep Problems

Most of the people who have a problem catching sleep usually do so out of physical or psychological health conditions. Anxiety can also make a person lose sleep or wake up in the middle of the night and worry until morning. For instance, an impending job interview, press conferences or even holiday trips can create anxiety. Many of the people who suffer from generalized anxiety disorders experience sleep problems.

Muscle Tension

Whether you are constantly clenching your jaws, flexing your muscles all over your body or balling your fists, this could be a sign of anxiety disorders. This problem can be pervasive and so consistent that people who have been suffering from it may think that it is normal and therefore not take any steps or seek medical attention.

Regular exercise can help you to ease the muscle tension and you should always avoid situations that will flare up your tension and disrupt your workout habits.

Chronic Indigestion

Even though anxiety is mental oriented, it can manifest itself in physical form such as chronic indigestion. Research has indicated that irritable bowel syndrome (IBS) which is usually characterized by cramping, gas, bloating, stomachaches, diarrhea and constipation is a sign of anxiety. The gut is usually sensitive to any instance of psychological stress and at the same time social and physical discomfort of the digestive tract can make a person anxious.

Panic Attacks

When you experience frequent panic attacks a sudden feeling of helplessness and other scary physical symptoms such as a racing heart, breathing problems, sweating, feeling of numbness, stomach pain and dizziness, you could be having an anxiety disorder.

It is not always that a person who has these signs suffers from anxiety disorder but chances are very high that such a person may be diagnosed with anxiety disorders. People with panic attacks always live in fear concerning events of the future and how they may unfold.

Perfectionism

Perfectionism which is a major symptom of obsessive-compulsive disorder (OCD) usually goes hand in hand with anxiety disorders. The moment you find yourself overly judgmental about your affairs, feel anticipatory anxiety about falling short of expectations or making mistakes then you may be suffering from anxiety disorder.

For instance, there are cases of people who cannot get out of the house for hours until the clothes or the makeup they have worn is perfect and befits their own view of beauty and style. They keep on starting all over again in cycles because of an irrational fear.

The reason why anxiety exist in people is because it has a special relationship with the fight or flight reaction. People suffering from anxiety disorders may be less likely to die from accidents because they may not take the risk in the first place.

However, this problem of risk averseness can cripple you and tie you in a mental corner where you may not get much out of life. You need to step up and start facing your anxiety and related conditions with a bold face knowing that you can overcome it regardless of its root cause.

3: The Response of the Mind and Body to Anxiety

The mind is the most powerful organ in human beings including animals. It can process millions of thoughts within a faction of a second. In the face of anxiety or anticipated danger, the fight and flight reactions come into full swing and they are extremely powerful.

Whenever people become frightened, the body including the mind goes through a series of steps that are aimed at protecting and strengthening the body so that it can overcome the obstacles at hand.

At times, the reaction is a mixture of both fear and anxiety. For instance, a person who is running for their lives because of a real danger such as a ranging storm may have both fear of the storm and anxiety due to possible destruction of property should the storm hit his home.

It is common to see such individuals having heart palpitations and an enhanced heartbeat. It is these reactions that begin from the mind that are associated with symptoms such as stomachs, nausea, muscle weakness, chest pain, hyperventilation and a lowered immune system.

When fear finally finds its way into your mental chambers, blood shifts from the prefrontal cortex part of the brain which is in charge of rational activities into the periaqueductal gray area which is responsible for survival responses. This explains why a person who is in a state of fear or panic may not reason in a rational way however much you try to calm them down. The simple reason is that there is insufficient blood in the logical area of the brain to enable it to function well.

Anxiety, panic and depressions are usually associated with an imbalance of chemicals in the brain namely dopamine, norepinephrine and serotonin.

The Contribution of Amygdala and Hippocampus to Anxiety

According to studies done on this subject matter, there appears to be a connection between the neural circuitry of the hippocampus and amygdala and anxiety.

The Amygdala and the Role It Plays in Anxiety

Amygdala refers to a mass of nuclei that is almond-shaped and located within the temporal lobe of the brains system. It is responsible with many of our motivations and emotions especially when it comes to survival. This part of the brain processes emotions such as anger, fear and pleasure. It is this part of the brain that also determines the kind of memories that are stored and where exactly they will be stored in the brain system.

Usually, the magnitude of emotional response that an event invokes determines to a larger extent where it will be stored on the brain. The amygdala plays a very crucial role in anxiety control in that it initiates arousals, emotional responses, autonomic responses associated with fear and hormonal secretions.

The Contribution of Hippocampus to Anxiety

The hippocampus is a section of the mind that is primarily concerned with the formation of memories, organizing of those memories and storing them. It is particularly responsible for connecting senses and emotions such as smell and sound to memories.

There is a hippocampus on either side of the brain hemisphere; the left and the right. The hippocampus functions as a memory indexer which sends out memories to the appropriate section of the cerebral hemisphere so that they can be stored for a long time and be retrieved where necessary. It contributes significantly in cases of anxiety especially where the anxiety is caused by flashbacks and events that happened in the past.

Research Findings

A study done at the University of Iowa in the laboratory of John Wemmie showed a correlation between the carbon dioxide and the metabolic factors of pH in the response to fear. The same study also showed that people with panic disorders will most likely experience a panic attack whenever they inhale air that contains 35 percent carbon dioxide concentration. This was not the case with people who did not have a panic disorder.

The studies about the response of the mind to anxiety have helped in the development of medications against anxiety disorders. The focus has now changed to addressing the acidity issue more than it was previously. Through exercise, meditation, yoga and other techniques, the pH balance of amygdala can be improved. This is achieved through a correction of the level of carbon dioxide in the mind and body.

4: Making Positive Use of Anxious Energy

The energy generated during scenarios of anxiety can be harnessed in a positive way to enhance progress instead of impeding it. For instance, if you consider the different attributes found in people with anxiety disorders, you will immediately discover that anxiety is not necessarily a terrible thing. It can be useful if you cast it in the right light. The energy that is poured when one imagines of worst case scenarios, can be carefully redirected and turned into positive energy to undertake constructive tasks.

Turn Anxiety into Creativity

People with anxiety, panic disorders and phobias usually have huge potentials for creativity that can be harvested from their catastrophic thinking. This is because for you to imagine a scenario that has not as yet happened and modeling it to a point where it seems real, it takes a lot of creativity, planning and visualization. Such are the minds of movie makers.

Take a Chance at Serving Others

In addition to creativity, people who suffer from anxiety tend to be more emphatic and self conscious than others. This is another attribute that can be turned around and used to steer a social agenda such as visiting the sick, organizing charities, participating in walks and activities that foster social justice.

Instead of locking yourself up and thinking what you want, it would do you good if you thought deeply about how you could serve others. When you serve others, you tap into feel good energy that can lift you from your current situation of anxiety and depression into a more pleasurable experience.

Wake up each day with a resolve to do something for the world either through your environment, your family or yourself. Always think about how you can be of value to other people and in this way, the entire gusto of anxious energy will be redirecting into a positive sensation.

Use Your Imagination to Engineer Your Success

In order to turn a particular feeling or fear into positive energy, you first need to understand it and what underlies it. Once you know about the feeling, you can then figure out how you would feel if that particular sensation was either absent or was turned into a positive experience.

Thereafter, you need to make a deliberate move and break from the jinx of the negative anxious energy and instead choose to live in a positive way. For instance, if you are feeling uneasy and cannot stay indoors, then you can take that opportunity and either take a walk or just jog around your yard so as to make the most out of that feeling. This will create a positive vibration that will lift your mood and calm you down.

Make Positive Affirmations

Whenever you find yourself in an anxious situation, you need to understand that the stress you could be experiencing is as a result of the situation that is at hand. In itself, the situation does not have power to cause stress and all it wants is to make you a victim of unwarranted anxiety. The best move in this case is to respond in such a manner as to enhance your energy and improve your health so that instead of becoming a victim to the situation, you can turn the stressor into a trigger for self development and improvement.

However severe the situation is, you need to boldly face it and say within yourself that you can manage it and you are stronger than it is. Remember affirmations generate positive energy of invincibility.

Enhance the Degree of Self Awareness

Anxiety is usually accompanied by moments of self consciousness and risk averseness. During these times, you tend to concentrate more on yourself and the impression you will project before people. Instead of letting this sensation of anxiety imprison you, you can turn it around for your own personal benefit. Use this energy to analyze your life and your body such as what you eat, your fashion preferences, your environment and even your posture. By concentrating on yourself, you will be able to unearth positive things about you that you are not previously aware of. You will also feel more confident and in control which is healthy for personal development.

Anticipate and Plan for Your Stressors

So as to benefit from anxious energy, you have to recognize that you can predict your stressors for a given day well in advance. This will give you time to prepare for them so that the moment they occur, you have gathered enough momentum to stop them. By dealing with your stressors in advance, you can preempt them by maintaining a positive posture and a very strong belief stand that you can succeed in everything that you do. Many times people are caught unawares by stressors and therefore depend on sheer luck to sail through making them victim of their stressors.

Free yourself of Unnecessary Baggage

Life is a journey that is like a voyage ship carrying cargo from one destination to the next. For you to succeed and sail through, you only have to carry the cargo that befits your capacity so as not to sink your ship below the Plimsoll line. This will need vigilance and self consciousness so that you can only take in and tag along issues that you can honestly bear.

For instance, you need to ask yourself whether you need all the baggage you are carrying, whether you must work all the time or you can take some time off among other strategic questions. By limiting the things that you load your mind with, you can successfully unshackle yourself and enhance your power.

If it is necessary, you can walk away from issues that trigger anxiety. You can stop going to meetings that add no value to your life. The energy and stress that could have resulted from these situations will be spared and used for your personal benefit. The moment you ditch the excess cargo, you will discover the incredible feeling of being light and how easy it is to accomplish your life purpose.

Throughout history, people have suffered from anxiety both prominent and laymen alike. The good thing is that they have managed to turn their travails into successes.

5: Psychotherapy - How It Can Help Anxiety

Psychotherapy is the most effective way of dealing with issues of anxiety. Whether to see a psychotherapist or not can be a tough decision that must be informed by the self assessments checklists and questionnaires discussed previously.

A therapist is more of a friend who sees the world from your perspective and will do everything to pull you out from your anxiety condition. He will help you to change certain habits which could be the main cause of anxiety.

Through a stepwise approach consisting of unawareness, self awareness and recognition, he will help you to deal with your situation in a strategic manner. For instance, he may analyze your eating habits so as to get a clue of how healthy your diet is.

When choosing a psychologist or a therapist, you need to work with someone that you are comfortable with so that you can achieve progress. The psychologist will help you in facing the difficult times and moments of discomfort and will show you how to move through them instead of just walking away without any tangible solution.

Types of Psychotherapy

There are many schools of psychotherapy and they differ in both form and substance. Not all of them will be appropriate for your condition and choosing one over the other needs understanding of how each works.

Cognitive Behavioral Therapy (CBT)

This is the most common psychotherapeutic approach that is used in the management and address of anxiety disorders. It involves intense focus on the present situations and dealing with the behaviors and fears that result.

What the CBT therapist will do first is to discuss with you the issues that are going on in your life and the kinds of fears that are underlying your problems. He will help you to restructure the manner in which you respond to the different stimuli. This type of psychotherapy does not look back through your childhood experiences but rather is much interested in the issues that are affecting you today.

CBT is very effective in that the treatment it advances involves exposure therapy. This type of therapy addresses fears and phobias and how to overcome them by exposing yourself to the trigger in a safe environment.

When going through exposure therapy, it is very important that you have a professional who will guide you throughout the experience. For instance, if you are afraid of water (hydrophobia), exposure therapy will introduce you to the same water that you are fearing through a gradual process that involves reprogramming of the mind so that it can respond differently in the face of the stimuli.

The Six Phases of Cognitive Behavioral Therapy

There are six phases or stages that comprise the process of CBT. These are discussed below:

- *Assessment*

  In this phase, you understand what your fears and phobias are and the impact they have in your life.

- *Re-conceptualization*

  This phase is aimed at changing your perception towards the fear inducing stimuli.

- ***Skills Acquisition***

  In this phase of CBT, the goal is to help you in developing specific skills that will enhance your ability to overcome anxieties and fears.

- ***Skills Consolidation and Training***

  The skills acquired in the above phase are put to work in a very efficient and effective manner.

- ***Maintenance***

  In this phase, you will learn how to develop habits and maintain the skills you have attained so that they can help you in the management of anxiety so as to progress in life.

- ***Assessment Follow-up***

  This is the last phase of CBT and it involves checking in and assessing whether the skills are still working and if any new problems have surfaced.

Freudian Psychoanalysis

This is the type of psychotherapy that many people imagine of whenever they think about visiting a therapist office. In practice, Freudian analysis is a broad term that has different approaches under it. However as a whole, Freudian analysis works by letting the patient discuss their inner dreams, thoughts, free associations and fantasies and thereafter the psychologist will be able to interpret all this and draw a conclusion about the underlying roots of the problems. Unlike CBT which focuses on the solutions, Freudian psychoanalysis examines the causes behind the anxiety disorder.

The Six Tenets of Traditional Psychoanalysis

- The emotional development of a person is largely determined by the events and experiences they had in early childhood.

- Human behavior and thought patterns depend on irrational drives.

- The irrational drives that usually motivate human behavior are mostly unconscious.

- Any attempt to bring unconscious drives to conscious awareness will be met by a rise in defense mechanisms.

- Whenever the unconscious and the conscious conflict, mental disturbances usually result including anxiety, neurosis, panic, depression among others.

- Acknowledgement by the conscious mind will help in freeing it from the effects of the unconscious drives.

Group Therapy

Depending on the guiding psychologists, group therapy can be closely associated with analytic therapy and cognitive behavioral therapy. In group therapy, one or more therapists usually lead a group of people with anxiety disorder through a session together.

The advantage of group therapy is that it enables the patients to share their experiences making them feel less alone and comforted. When you hear the stories of other people, you will feel motivated and supported as opposed to the case of one on one therapy where the therapists focuses only on your own fears.

Group therapy can also coincide with exposure therapy. For example, if you suffer from social anxiety, group therapy can help you to face and overcome your fears by exposing you to a safe environment. However, the introduction to group therapy for people who suffer from social anxiety should be done gradually because their fear of social situations may make them to resist participation or to clam up.

Family Therapy

This is a combination of family counseling and couple therapy. The good thing with this kind of therapy is that the people involved are those that are close to you. This helps you in opening up and also in addressing the impact of the anxiety disorder and its underlying stimuli within the family. Family therapy opens doors for interpersonal support systems and gives an opportunity for family members to express their fears, individual frustrations and motivations.

Family and couple therapy can foster a healthy relationship and communication path with your loved ones thereby promoting a deeper understanding of fear and anxiety.

How to Choose a Therapist

After the introduction of the common branches of psychotherapy above and a brief discussion of how each one of them works, the first task that you have when choosing a therapist is deciding on the approach that will serve you best.

This is not an issue of mathematical computation but may involve you gut instinct. Some forms of therapy will work best compared to others for a certain group of people. For instance, if you feel that one on one therapist will be better than a group therapist, then go for it. The following resources can help you start your search for a credible therapist.

The Anxiety and Depression Association of America is a body that has an excellent resource page (www.adaa.org) for psychologists who specialize in depression and anxiety within the United Sates.

The American Psychiatric Association (www.psych.org) and the American Psychological Association (www.apa.org) provide comprehensive lists of medical practitioners and therapists.

Family and friends can give you some commendable referrals to therapists who have a good industry reputation. Mental health issues and anxiety disorders usually have a social stigma meaning you need to talk to trusted family members and friends to avoid being the gossip of the town. You can strike a rapport with a person who is already seeing a therapist so that you can ask them for a referral.

A managed care company or an insurance agency can have complete lists of therapists which can be availed to you depending on the plan you have subscribed to.

Local colleges and universities usually have brilliant resources that you can always check. If the college has a psychiatry or psychology department then you can ask them for recommendations on the best therapists available.

Assessing the Appropriateness of Your Therapist

The moment you find a therapist that you are comfortable with, you can go ahead and make an appointment for a consultative session. Before stepping in for the consultation, you need to prepare adequately and if possible make a list of assessments and questions that you can use.

You need to ask the therapists about their history specifically concerning the duration they have been in the practice and the frequency with which they deal with people suffering from anxiety disorders. They also need to tell you how the patients who have gone through their hands are fairing today.

The other thing that you need to ask them is in relation to their policies. You can ask them the fees they charge for every single session and the payment plan available. You will also have to find out about the frequency with which they schedule their sessions and whether they offer one on one or group therapy only.

Assess the background of the therapist and more so look for instances where there were breaches to professionalism and confidentiality. Be particularly concerned with therapists who have pending legal proceedings for matters associated with their profession.

Once you go through these steps, you should be comfortable with the therapist that you settle for. Remember that discomfort feelings are part and parcel of therapies but you should feel comfortable with the psychologist himself.

You need to find someone that you trust. Feel free to discuss with the therapist other techniques that you plan to implement or are implementing in your anxiety management program. If there are any techniques that they can suggest you try, it can also be very helpful.

6: The Power of Meditation and Its Benefits

Meditation is one of the ancient practices that have proved effective with time when it comes to controlling and managing anxiety. According to studies done, people who meditate extensively rarely get entrapped in phobias, anxiety, depression and panic disorders.

Meditation helps in eliminating your breathing dysfunction and is effective in centering your body, mind and spirit. There are many different types of meditation but the common one is known as Transcendental Meditation.

Transcendental Meditation

This is a form of meditation that was developed by Maharishi Mahesh Yogi and was slowly adopted in the western world becoming popular in the 1960s and 1970s. It uses a mantra or sound and is usually practiced in sessions that last about 20 minutes each two times a day. Despite the fact that Transcendental Meditation has roots in the Hindu beliefs, it does not involve any apparent religious practices.

More than 600 studies have been conducted to analyze the effects of Transcendental Meditation. Each of the studies has continuously reaffirmed that meditation improves the emotional, cognitive and physical effects of anxiety and stress.

The best part is that unlike conventional medicine, meditation does not have side effects and do not demand much restructuring of your way of life. The cost involved in meditation is also comparatively low when compared with other anxiety disorder management approaches.

Benefits of Meditation in Anxiety Management

Meditation as an exercise of the mind is effective in enhancing the quality of life by working wholesomely on your mental, emotional and physical attributes. There are as many benefits of meditation as there are meditation techniques. Below are some of the benefits that you can derive from meditative processes to help you fight anxiety and related tendencies.

Enhances Your Mood

Meditation helps us to face life problems with an inner resolve and capacity rather than shying away from them. At any point in life, everyone faces stressful situations that can easily lead us down the path of depression and anxiety.

Whether it is school, work or family life, we need to deal with the circumstances in such a manner that we control the cause of action instead of becoming victims. Even when working under extreme pressure, meditation has been proved through scientific studies to be effective in reversing negative moods, chronic stress and anxiety.

Reduces the Level of Mental Distractions

Anxiety usually takes the mind off the focus making you disoriented. By training the mind to concentrate on a particular process or task you can achieve more and become productive in whatever you do. According to scans done on the brain matter, there is evidence that experience in meditation makes it easy to process distracting thoughts so as to quickly return to a stable and focused state of mind.

The good thing is that the rewards of meditation do not take long to come by as some people take as little as a week to improve their cognitive abilities and reduce stress.

Meditation Improves the Size of Your Brain

Although it may look trivial, an improved brain size is beneficial in the fight against anxiety. As you age, the frontal cortex thins making you more vulnerable to instances of anxiety and stress. Meditation helps in growing the gray matter through mental exercise. This is the portion of the brain tissue that is responsible for cognition, language and emotional response.

Boosts Immune System

The body immunity is positively correlated with emotional stability. The higher the immune system, the more stable you are emotionally. One of the key strategies in fighting anxiety is to attain stability in your emotional make up.

According to a study carried out on meditators and non-meditators, it was found that meditators had more antibodies in their blood system compared to their non-meditating counterparts. In the same study, it was also observed that there was increased activity in the sections of the brain that are associated with positive emotions.

Meditation Helps in Alleviating Symptoms of Health Problems

Stress affects the ability of our body immunity to fight diseases. When we become anxious, phobic and depressed, chances of developing illnesses such as high blood pressure and heart diseases are very high. Meditation can help in alleviating the symptoms caused by these conditions and at the same time reduce the level of stress and anxiety so as to completely do away with the health conditions.

Meditation Decreases Fatigue

Instead of going for a cup of coffee as a stimulant, you can decide to settle for meditation which has even greater stimulation benefits. Meditation is effective in making your mind alert thereby increasing your performance by reducing unnecessary sessions of sleep. Because fatigue can cause anxiety, stopping it before it takes its toll on you can be an effective way to fight anxiety from its root.

Helps in Reducing the Impact of Emotional Pain

Emotional pain accompanied by negative thinking can degenerate into a mental problem and in some instances stress. Studies have indicated that meditation can reduce events of emotional pain up to 50%. Your response to emotional pain can also be much more structured if you have a habit of regularly meditating.

Enhances Your Social Interactivity

Meditation creates a powerful force that breaks the barriers of isolation and inferiority complex thereby helping you to freely interact with other people. Social anxiety is a type of disorder that makes it increasingly difficult to mingle with other people and creates some sort of discomfort whenever you force yourself to do it.

By going into meditation, you can be able to increase your level of appreciation for other people and your self-acceptance metrics which are crucial in fostering social interactions.

How to Get Started with Meditation

In order to start a successful meditation program, you need to locate a good meditation center that has knowledgeable instructors. These resources are all over and even on the internet. You can also buy audio books and subscribe you to videos that will guide you through the process of meditation.

You need to find the right place and time to do your meditations in sessions of about 20 minutes each. Ensure that during your meditation time, the environment is quiet and free from destruction. You should turn off radios, televisions, cell phones and any other devices that could interrupt you.

You can also get into a comfortable position which is not necessary the full-lotus position. You can lie down, sit, stand or even walk. When breathing in during meditation, use your nose and breathe out using your mouth. Even if you do not notice changes immediately, you need to realize that meditation is an ongoing process and may take a while for the effects to crystallize.

7: Positive Visualizations

Positive visualization is effective in stopping your mind from catastrophic thinking. It also includes some elements of meditation. Positive visualization is also used as a daily relaxation activity as well as a technique in stopping yourself from careening into the depths of panic and anxiety. The key to undertaking successful positive visualization lies in the specifics; you have to take much time and go through each detail of your journey.

Locate a Quiet Place that is Free of Distractions

A visualization session should be held in a place that is relatively quiet with fewer human activities or none at all. If you decide to do it at home, you can choose to lie on the floor, on your bed or sit in a yoga blanket or mat. Distractions can make you uncomfortable and as such you should close your eyes so as to lock yourself in your own world.

Focus on Your Breathing Pattern

So as to start the relaxation process, you need to first of all examine your breathing in the same manner you would do when meditating. Ensure that you feel the inhaled air as it expands your lungs, flows into your abdomen and lowers your diaphragm. Take a few minutes to just focus on your breathing only. If thoughts enter your mind during this period, all you need to do is just acknowledge them and stop being harsh on yourself. Every exhalation should be seen as a release of air from your body system.

Start Focusing on a Specific Body Part

While still breathing, slowly direct your thoughts to a certain area of your body. This can be your feet, hands, ears and any other part that you may want to start with. Handle one part at a time and move in a gradual manner. Assuming you started with the feet, you need to ask yourself about the sensations you feel in your toes, ankles and the heels of your feet. If you are wearing socks, you need to visualize how the material feels on your skin.

Breathe into Each Body Area

As you still focus on your feet and breathing, you need to imagine your breathe spreading and stretching all the way to your feet. You can decide to tense and then relax your feet so as to specify your sensations. While doing this, you need to imagine that every stream of breathe has healing light.

This light is gradually passed from your mouth to your throat, down to your lungs and then expands to every part of the body. After the feet, you need to continue with the journey to other parts of the body. If stray thoughts find their way into your mind at this stage, you need to acknowledge them and proceed.

Starting the Visualization Process

After you go through each part of the body, you can now relax and breathe. This is the point where your visualization starts because the body is warmed up and ready for the exercise. There is no wrong and correct way for visualization because it is whatever will make you the happiest, most relaxed and comfortable.

You can decide to visualize a peaceful and quiet setting on an island. You can also decide to envision yourself being announced the winner of a lottery, getting married or securing a promotion at the workplace. At this stage, the mind will create a positive feeling. You should also note that you may not get a perfect and ideal visualization on the first day but you should not stop at that point but rather forge ahead.

The nature of the visualization does not matter as much but what is of importance is how clearly you imagine it and the impact it creates in your body and mind.

Indulge in Specifics

Whether the imagined situation is real or just a fantasy, you need to capture every detail of it. For instance the taste of the air, its warmth and the things you are touching in your imagined setting. Allow your mind to crisscross and wander through the imagined scenario and pick everything in it; the smell, the sound, the sight, the textures and the emotions. All these will contribute to how you will feel at the end of the process.

Gradually Return to Reality

Give yourself enough time to spend at your imagined scenario and the moment you are ready to return to reality, all you need is just to refocus your thoughts to your breathe. You can now breathe slowly and deliberately and this should take you back to where you began. You can revisit your legs, back, chest and hands as you return to your starting point. After the process, ensure that you do not rush in getting up because some areas of your body may still be in relaxation mode.

8: Sleep and Relaxation Techniques

Adequate sleep is necessary for the body to rest and rejuvenate from day to day hassles and stresses. It is a major factor that influences the working of your mind and by extension, your anxiety level. When you are anxious, you are likely to experience lack of sleep because your mind is taken through a cycle that anticipates possible dangers. Your lack of sleep will in turn cause another round of even more severe anxiety and emotional frailty.

Even though sleep is addressed in meditation, it is important to consider it as a separate subject matter and work towards promoting its quality. You need to establish a daily routine that will define your sleeping and waking up times. This will condition your body in such a way that no amount of stress or anxiety can interfere with your deeply entrenched discipline of sleeping and waking up.

Free Your Bedroom from Distractions

This is the first approach that you need to boldly make so as to attain a quality rest to boost your health and lower your anxiety. Try as much as possible to avoid putting or installing televisions, radios or computers in your bedroom. You need to reserve it for rest and relaxation only. The only gadgets that you can allow are alarm clocks because you need them for waking up.

Establish a Routine for Bedtime

Give yourself like an hour so as to prepare adequately for bed. During this time, ensure that you let go of family worries, work worries and any other thoughts that could be troubling and nagging your mind. It is inappropriate to go to bed with all these baggage in your head.

In order to promote relaxation, you can take a warm bath or soak your feet in warm water. Depending on your preferences, you can choose to light some aromatic candles to sooth you as you adjust for bedtime. Keep off any household chores and simply relax.

Take Some Soothing Literature as You Settle in Bed

In order to lull yourself to sleep, you can take a good book with you or a crossword puzzle that will challenge and inspire your mind. Do not take a novel that you will not be able to put down once you start reading. Self-help books and inspirational books can be excellent as you wind down to sleep.

Sit or Lie in a Comfortable Position

When you go to bed, you need to be careful about your posture. If you are reading a book, the best posture will be to sit as opposed to lying down. This is because reading while lying down will create tension in your muscles which is very bad and can cause stress.

When lying on your bed, ensure that you can feel your breath as well as your abdomen as you breathe. Your hands and feet should be uncrossed so that they too can relax. Ensure that the pillow you choose is not hard and also not too soft. A hard pillow will press hard against your neck causing it to strain while a pillow that is too soft will give in to your weight creating a depression that will in turn destabilize your posture.

Maintain a Sleeping Journal

As you lie and relax in bed, there are some thoughts and feelings that will come to you. Whenever such cross your mind, you need to take out your notebook and write them down. Do not judge yourself harshly because this may worsen the situation. Just put everything down on pen and paper as this can be an opportunity to release your fears through words.

In order to boost your chances of getting quality sleep, you can include a meditation session before you sleep or engage in some exercises during the day. Remember that the better you sleep the more confident and resolved you will be in managing your anxiety and facing the following day.

9: Effective Methods to Tricking Your Mind

Mind tricking is effective in dealing with immediate panic and anxiety instances. There are certain times when panic attacks come and you are not prepared. This could be the case when you are travelling. During such instances, you need to trick or deceive your mind in some way so that you can attain calmness. Some of the practices you can use include:

Count Your Breath

Just like it is in meditation, counting your breath can help in calming you thereby enabling you to refocus your mind on the present issues. You can count your breath silently when you are in a train, bus or a plane without anyone knowing what you are up to. For instance, you can choose the number 100 and count up to it repeatedly in sets of 10 breaths. While counting, your feelings of anxiety will slowly subside thereby creating a relief.

Mini Positive Visualization

This is a shortcut that you can resort to so as to enable you attain positive visualization. All you need to do is choose a point of focus such as a small hole on the ground or a doorknob. Try as much as possible to avoid choosing a person as your point of focus because this can bring a confrontation.

The moment you settle on a given spot, ensure that you focus your eyes right there and let your mind envision a comfortable and safe place. It will be easier for this exercise to work if you have practiced the full version of positive visualization. You can imagine the warmth of sunlight on your face, a cool breeze coming from the sea and any other desirable thing that you want.

Play a Mental Game

As you wait in long lines to board a bus or train, you can avoid feeling anxious by playing some mind games. These games take the mind off from the present situation and immerse it in the game that you are playing. One of the easiest games you can play is naming a city for every letter of the alphabet. Also, you can count the number plates of the vehicles that are passing on the road.

Puzzles and hobbies

You can decide to fill crossword puzzles or Sudoku puzzles. These activities however little they may seem can stop your mind from plunging into a situation of anxiety. They tend to refocus it on the task at hand therefore preventing anxiety.

Calling a Friend

Whether you are at work or travelling in the bus, you can decide to pick up your phone and call a friend. The effect of this is that the moment you hear the reassuring voice of a person you trust, your anxiety level will start going down. If you want to discuss your fears with a friend, you can go ahead but it is not a must. Some people experience calmness the moment they see their therapists.

These are just some of the ways through which you can deal with panic and anxiety in immediate situations. One thing you should note is that these methods are just temporal and may not sustain you into the future. What you need to do is to use them in conjunction with the other methods that were discussed earlier in the book.

You always need to be open and discuss other ways of managing panic and anxiety with your therapists. There are several other tricks that you can play on your mind but not all of them will be effective. You need to choose the ones that fit your individual case.

10: Alternative Methods of Anxiety Management

This chapter discusses the less traditional ways through which you can manage stress and anxiety. These methods are referred to as alternative because they are less scientifically researched compared to the other techniques that have been discussed in the previous chapters.

Nevertheless, these methods are gaining recognition among the people who battle anxiety disorders. In most cases, these alterative techniques are combined with the mainstream anxiety management methods such as yoga, meditation and nutrition so as to enhance your mood making you happier and calmer.

Aromatherapy

This refers to the practice of using essential oils that are scented so as to affect your mood. Aromatherapy helps in creating an atmosphere of calmness and serenity which is effective in managing anxiety. Because of its effectiveness, manufacturers of shampoos, scented soaps, perfumes, scented candles and room fresheners have incorporated the concept of aromatherapy. Some of the practices that aromatherapy works well with is meditation, calming bathes and visualization. Some of the essential oils to look out for include:

- ***Ylang Ylang***

  This is an essential oil that is derived from the flowers of a perfume tree. It is effective in relieving high blood pressure and normalizing skin problems. Its calming effect will help you in getting rid of stress and anxiety.

- ***Bergamot***

  This type of essential oil is extracted from the Bergamot orange tree that grows in the southern part of Italy and France. The scent of Bergamot is uplifting and can be used to calm frazzled nerves.

- ***Sandalwood***

  This is harvested from the Sandalwood tree. The essential oil has a woody and musky scent that helps in creating a calming effect on the nervous system. Many religious rituals in Japan, India and China use the sandalwood oils.

- ***Chamomile***

This essential oil has a sweet and fruity scent. It is derived from the chamomile flower. The oil is usually used as an ingredient in making chamomile tea that is effective in relieving stress and calming the mind.

- ***Lavender***

Lavender is extracted from the mint family and is associated with stress relief. It can also be incorporated in scented candles, perfumes and bath salts.

- ***Geranium Rose***

This is a flower that is commonly used in the perfume industry and it is cultivated in South Africa. It is great for creating a smoothing and calming atmosphere which is necessary for balancing of hormones.

These are just some of the common essential oils that are used in relieving stress and lowering anxiety levels. There are many more fragrances that can give you an excellent sensation and relaxation feeling. This area is open for research as more and more oils are unveiled through scientific researches and tests.

Hypnotherapy

This method was founded by Dr. John Kappas who is also the founder of the Hypnosis Motivation Institute. Usually, hypnotherapy involves the induction of hypnotic state into a client so as to alter behavior patterns or increase motivation. The client is first explained to on how hypnosis works and the experience they will go through.

Hypnotherapy is effective in addressing anxiety disorders and their underlying fears. It is often used alongside cognitive behavioral therapy as an approach to exposure therapy. Today, hypnotherapy has been accepted and implemented by psychiatrists and therapists in managing depression, anxiety, phobias, addiction and insomnia.

Acupuncture

The origin of acupuncture is ancient China and involves the insertion of tiny needles into acupuncture points located on the skin. The logic behind this method lies in the lilies of pent-up energy from the meridians of the body thereby creating balance.

Scientific studies undertaken on traditional acupuncture have found out that the practice is effective in relieving nausea and pain. In the United States, acupuncturists usually attend an accredited program that last for about 3 to 4 years in order to become licensed.

When looking for an acupuncturist, you have to ensure that you go for someone who has the qualifications, has an excellent history of satisfied patients and is also licensed to undertake the practice. Sham acupuncturists can do you more harm than good.

Alternative methods of anxiety management are therefore very effective and are gaining prominence gradually as people expand beyond the conventional practices in order to embrace these techniques. They are commonly incorporated as part of total healing processes.

Conclusion

Anxiety is a very common condition in the society today and every one of us becomes anxious at one point or another. Changes in lifestyles have a tremendous impact in the way our minds perceive and process instances of stress. Over the past 50 years or so, westerners have gone through a cycle that has seen a massive overhaul in the way people play, work, interact with one another and maintain wellness. Even though change is welcome, it can induce stress if it is not handled in the proper manner.

People have had to adjust to an environment that is characterized by smart technology such as Smartphones, smart televisions, increased internet connectivity and the influence of an overly aggressive media that has contributed positively to the rising cases of panic and anxiety disorders.

Societal transitions lead to anxiety by changing the way individuals live their lives. Evolutions in professions for instance have caused people to be retrenched while putting others on the lifeline as they fight tooth and nail to save their careers and jobs.

Such situations make a perfect case for anxiety and related disorders. As opposed to the popular view, admitting that you are suffering from anxiety is not a defeatist stand but rather a brave one and a show that you have accepted anxiety as part and parcel of your normal life.

How you manage anxiety can mean the difference between facing everyday problems with courage or leaving your home because of fear and panic.

Use the methods that have been put forward in this book as your starting point to a life of serenity and calmness even when you are at the eye of the storm. Take a few moments everyday where possible so that you can re-enter your body and your mind. This will make it easier for you to truly appreciate your family, friends and the world around you.

Your path to living a life that is free of anxiety may involve the services of a therapist or learning how to effectively schedule your time. Regardless of whatever it takes, you deserve a life that is full of happiness and devoid of fear.